ALLEN PHOTOG

GW01185320

ALL ABOUT
MANES AND TAILS

CONTENTS

SETTING THE SCENE	2
WHAT SUITS YOUR HORSE?	2
WHY PULL?	3
BRIDLEPATHS	3
PULLING A MANE	4
HOW TO PULL	4
PULLING AND BANGING TAILS	6
PULLING TECHNIQUES	6
KEEP IT EVEN	7
ALTERNATIVES TO PULLING	8
TRIMMING TECHNIQUES	8
THE RIGHT LENGTHS	9
CLEANING UP	10
WHEN TO WASH	10
BANDAGING TAILS	11
HOGGING A MANE	12
WHEN AND HOW TO HOG	12
PERFECT PLAITING	13
THE MANE DECISIONS	13
PLAITING TECHNIQUES	14
SEW PERFECT	14
BAND AID	18
RUNNING AND SPANISH PLAITS	19
THE RUNNING PLAIT	19
THE SPANISH PLAIT	20
PLAITING TAILS	21
PICK YOUR PLAIT	21
PLAITING TECHNIQUES	22

SETTING THE SCENE

WHAT SUITS YOUR HORSE?

A neatly pulled and/or plaited mane and tail can give the finishing touches to a horse's or pony's appearance. Before you start, check what fits in with your horse's lifestyle and type. One who lives out all the time needs extra protection so, rather than pulling his tail, you may prefer to leave it full and plait it for special occasions.

Breed societies and showing organisations have different rules about trimming and turnout which will affect you if you want to show. Native ponies are supposed to be shown in a natural state, but some societies accept judicious tidying. Pure-bred Arabs should have flowing manes and tails (*see bottom picture*), part-breds should be shown pulled and plaited and cobs traditionally have hogged manes.

If you do not know the breeding of your horse or pony, go by his type: hunter, cob, Mountain and Moorland and so on.

STAYING IN FASHION

Fashion affects the horse world, too. Some dressage riders like plaits fastened with white tape, but these would be out of place in the show ring. If in doubt, take the conservative approach. Fashion can be fickle!

WHY PULL?

Pulling a mane keeps it tidy and of a manageable length and thickness to plait. It is difficult to make symmetrical plaits from an uneven mane, and one that is too thick will give a row of golf balls along the neck!

A pulled tail is standard in the show ring, except for youngstock, and sets off the horse's hindquarters. A well-plaited tail does the same, but it is more difficult to plait a tail than a mane. A pulled tail, however, needs regular tidying and bandaging to keep it in shape – so it really is up to you.

BRIDLEPATHS

If you clip out a section of hair where the bridle headpiece goes, keep it small or you will have an ugly gap. Be equally cautious about clipping hair at the withers – taking off too much 'shortens' the horse's neck. It is considered incorrect to clip a bridlepath on a pure-bred native pony or Arab.

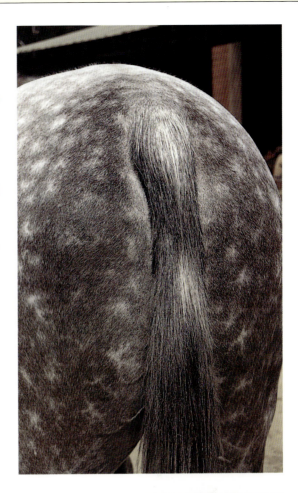

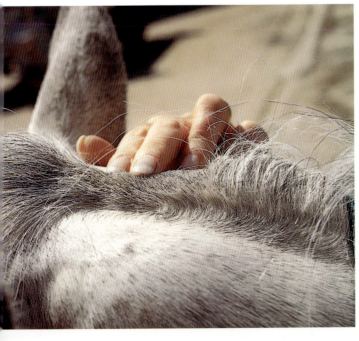

PULLING A MANE

HOW TO PULL

If you want to plait a mane, aim to pull it so that it is 4 or 5 in (10 or 12.5 cm) long and not too thick. Most horses do not mind having their manes and tails pulled if it is done considerately: this means working over several days if necessary.

The best time to pull is after exercise because the hairs will come out more easily when the horse is warm. If you work gradually over the whole area, rather than finishing a section at a time, the horse will not look odd.

You will need a well-lit working area where the horse can be tied up safely, or someone can hold him. For big horses, you may need something safe to stand on. If the horse is sensitive or an unknown quantity, wearing a hard hat and boots with protective toecaps minimises the risks resulting from being hit in the face or trodden on.

A metal pulling comb (1) has shorter teeth than a mane comb (2) and is the best thing to use (*see below left*). Sticking plaster over your finger joint stops you getting cut by horsehair.

Comb the mane to ensure there are no tangles and you can see how much to take out. Manes traditionally lie on the offside, but if it lies flat beautifully on the nearside you may prefer to follow rather than fight its natural inclinations.

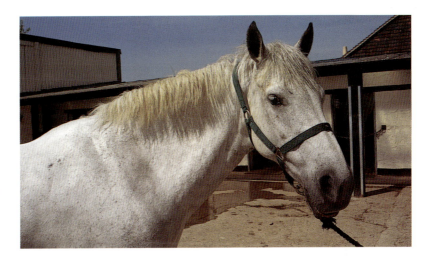

Always take hair from underneath – if you pull it from the top you end up with an untidy fringe growing down. Hold a few hairs at a time, push the comb along them to keep the top hair out of the way and pull out the underneath ones in one quick movement. If the hair does not come out easily, wrap it round the comb before you pull. Comb the mane down often and check that your line is even.

Never cut a mane with scissors. This leaves blunt ends and looks unnatural, unlike pulling.

COMFORT FIRST

Some horses are more relaxed if you pull out the hairs with an upward rather than a downward pull. Be especially careful when working near the ears, as many horses are more sensitive here than near the withers.

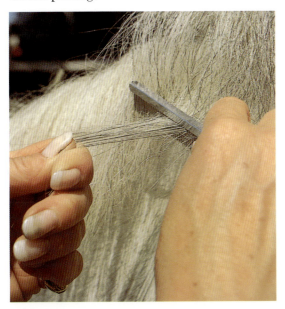

PULLING AND BANGING TAILS

PULLING TECHNIQUES

Pulling tails is potentially more dangerous as you have to stand in kicking range. Never underestimate the risks. Again, work over several days and when the horse is warm and relaxed.

If you know the horse kicks or are unsure of his reactions, build a straw bale barrier behind him. This, not you, will take the brunt if he kicks; this method is much safer and more practical than trying to pull a tail over a stable door.

When starting from scratch, use a pulling comb or a nylon one intended for human use if you find it easier. Use the same technique as with pulling a mane. Brush the tail through, then start at the top and take out a few underneath hairs from each side. Gradually work down until you reach about halfway down the dock.

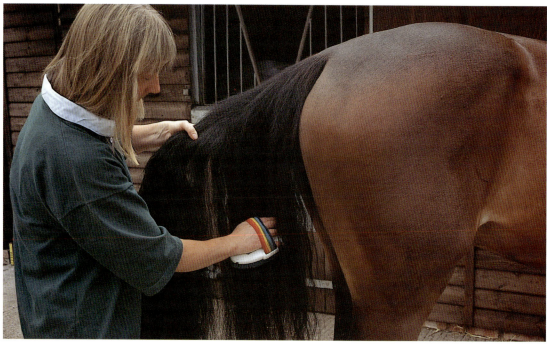

KEEP IT EVEN

It is easier to keep the shape of the tail symmetrical if you work on both sides at the same time, rather than finishing one side and then starting on the other. Be patient and take only a few hairs at a time from each spot, or you will end up with a bald patch.

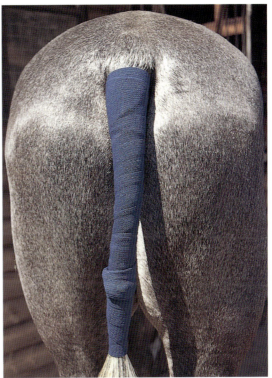

A fine tail is easier to pull than a coarse one with a thick dock. Often you will only need to take hair from the sides. With a thick tail, as found on most cobs, you may also need to pull from the centre.

Be careful not to pull too much hair from the centre at the top, or the top of the tail will look like a loo brush. Once you have finished, dampen the tail hair and put on a tail bandage for an hour or two. To keep a pulled tail in shape, you need to bandage it regularly. You will also need to tidy a pulled tail regularly. The easiest way to pull hairs that are too short to grasp is to get hold of them with a pair of square-nosed pliers. This enables you to pull hairs in one sharp action, which is more comfortable for the horse.

ALTERNATIVES TO PULLING

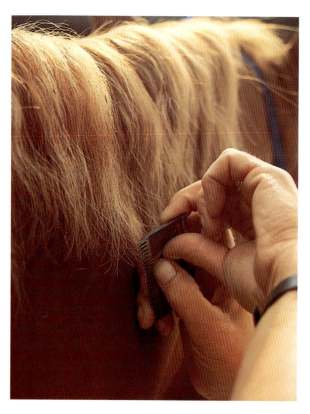

TRIMMING TECHNIQUES

Most horses accept having their manes and tails pulled if handled correctly and patiently but a few dislike it so much that it becomes risky.

Some horses – usually Thoroughbreds – have manes so fine that they need to be shortened but not thinned. In these cases, it is best to use trimming techniques.

You can either use a sharp clipper blade or a special comb which combines a comb and a blade. With manes, backcomb the hair and press down with the blade; the result looks much the same as pulling. With tails, trim three or four hairs at a time from the sides and, if necessary, the centre. Bandage the tail regularly to encourage the hairs to lie flat.

USING A TWITCH

Some horses settle better if you use a twitch. Applied correctly – and only to the top lip – it does not cause pain. Instead, it encourages the production of natural substances called endorphins which make the horse relaxed or even sleepy.

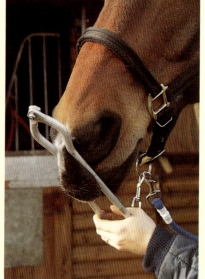

THE RIGHT LENGTHS

You may need to shorten as well as shape the tail. The smartest look, except when breed guidelines call for a natural look, is to bang the tail, i.e. cut it across to give a level bottom edge.

Before doing this it is important to see how the horse carries his tail on the move. If you bang it when he is standing still, it will be lopsided in action. Get someone to walk him so you can see his natural tail carriage. Then get a helper to put a hand under the dock and hold it at the same angle.

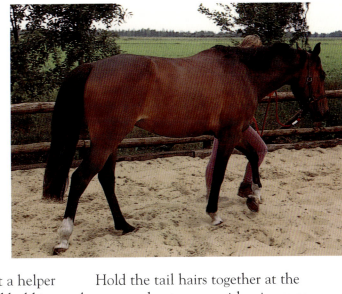

Hold the tail hairs together at the bottom and cut across with scissors or clippers. It is easier to get a straight line with clippers, especially on a thick tail.

The best length is usually 2 – 4 in (5 – 10 cm) below the point of the hock when the horse is moving. Those native ponies whose societies allow tidying up, usually have them longer so that the banged tail reaches the fetlocks.

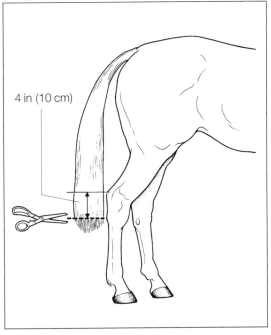

4 in (10 cm)

CLEANING UP

WHEN TO WASH

Horses produce grease, which looks like waxy dust, as a barrier against the rain. Whilst you would not want to bath a horse who lives out too often, because he needs this natural water-proofing agent, you can wash his mane and tail.

Use horse shampoo prepared according to the manufacturer's instructions: it usually needs to be dilut-ed. Do not use washing-up liquid as it may irritate the horse's skin.

Wet the hair well, preferably using a sponge and lukewarm water. Put the tail in a bucket of water to wet the long hairs, standing to one side in case the horse kicks out. Work in the shampoo, rubbing quite hard into the roots of the mane and the dock hairs.

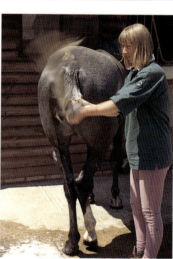

It is important to remove all the shampoo and the easiest way to do this is with a hosepipe. Most horses accept this if you are patient. After rinsing, to get rid of excess water from the tail, hold the dock with one hand and swish the long hairs round with the other.

WATER WARNINGS

Do not get sham-poo in the horse's eyes: pull the fore-lock back between his ears to wash it. If he will not accept a hose near his head, use plenty of clean water and a sponge.

BANDAGING TAILS

Applying a tail bandage after you have washed the tail will make the hair lie flat. A pulled tail should be bandaged regularly to train the hair to lie neatly. Use an elasticated bandage and dampen the hair but never the bandage; if you wet the bandage it will tighten as it dries and could restrict the circulation, resulting in injury. For the same reason, do not leave a tail bandage on overnight.

Unroll 6 – 8 in (15 – 20 cm) of bandage and put it under the tail. Make your first turn, fold down the loose end and bandage over it: this helps prevent slipping. Bandage down with even, firm, but not tight, pressure until you get to the end of the dock bones. Go back up, if necessary, then tie the tapes in a double bow no tighter than the tension of the bandage.

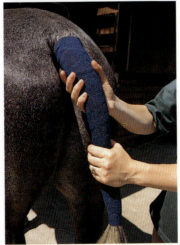

Tuck in the ends, folding the bandage over them if you prefer, and gently bend the tail into its natural position. To remove the bandage, simply undo the tapes, grasp the bandage with both hands at the top and slide it down and off.

HOGGING A MANE

WHEN AND HOW TO HOG

Show cobs and polo ponies traditionally have hogged (clipped off) manes. Hogging makes many thickset, more common animals look smarter because it shows off their workmanlike heads. However, a horse must have a reasonable neck and topline to look nice with a hogged mane. A weedy neck will look even weedier with no mane!

Remember that if you change your mind, a hogged mane takes at least a year to grow out and looks like a yard broom for some of the time. You may also need to give the horse extra protection against flies in the summer by using fly fringes and repellents.

You can only hog with clippers, so the horse must accept these. Battery clippers are usually quieter than electric ones. First clip up each side, being careful not to cut into the neck hair, then run the clippers along the centre.

With a strong neck, keep the line even, but to give the impression of more bulk, clip close near the withers and ears and leave a little more mane in the middle of the neck.

CLEAN LINES

A greasy hogged mane looks even worse than a greasy long one. Keep it clean by wiping it with a cloth dampened with surgical spirit or witch hazel.

PERFECT PLAITING

THE MANE DECISIONS

Traditionally, horses have seven or nine plaits up the neck and one for the forelock, stitched in place. However, it is now generally accepted that, within reason, there should be as many plaits as suits the horse's conformation.

There are many variations: plaiting with rubber bands, hunting plaits, stable plaits, plaiting with white tape and running plaits. Whatever type you choose, you need a reasonably clean but not newly washed mane to get the best results. Squeaky clean mane hair is slippery to handle and it is harder to keep the plaits taut as you work.

PLAITING TECHNIQUES

SEW PERFECT

To create immaculate plaits that stay in all day, you need to sew them in with a large darning needle and special plaiting thread. This is stronger than sewing thread and should match the colour of the horse's mane.

If you have never plaited before practise with three strands of wool or ribbon. Start by passing the right (green) strand over the centre (beige) one, then pass the left (brown) one over the new centre (green) strand. Carry on down the plait passing alternate strands over whatever has become the centre one.

Practice makes perfect. Professional show producers can plait a mane in fifteen to twenty minutes, though it may take some time to reach that standard.

Avoid plaiting in the stable. If you drop the needle you may have to remove all the bedding.

Try to plait on the day of your competition. If you have to plait the night before, the horse might rub his mane and there will certainly be bits of bedding to remove from the plaits next morning.

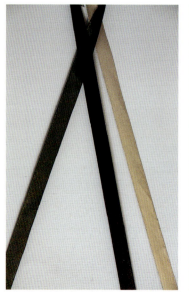

KEEPING CALM

Most horses show no objection to having their manes plaited, though some become bored with being tied up. Start near the ears, where most horses are more sensitive, and get the potentially ticklish bit over with first. Try not to brush the ears with your hand or the thread and protect the horse with fly repellent if necessary to minimise head shaking.

Comb the mane through and divide it into equal sections of roughly a mane comb's width (1). Some people find it easier if they keep the sections separate with rubber bands.

Dampen each section before you start plaiting: spraying the top of the section with hair gel helps prevent the inevitable short hairs at the top sticking up (2). Shield the other side of the neck with your hand to prevent the coat getting sticky.

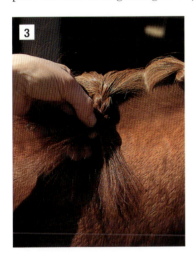

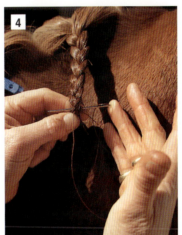

When you are ready to plait a mane, divide the section into three equal parts and keep the plait tight from the base (3). Plait as close to the end as you can, and either weave in the plaiting thread for the last inch or knot the cotton to stop it pulling through.

Pass the needle from the back to the front of the plait and secure the end (4) then turn over the end and wrap the thread round to keep the loose end hairs under control (5). This gives a better finish as it minimises the risk of loose hairs poking out from the base of the plait.

Now push the needle through the underside of the plait at the base so it doubles up (6). Roll up the plait to the neck and secure with a couple of stitches. If you want them to sit on top of the neck, push back as you stitch.

Continue down the neck, trying to keep each plait the same size. If there are loose hairs, spray them flat with hair gel or hairspray, but use your other hand to shield the top of the horse's neck so you do not get a sticky line down the other side. Do not be tempted to pull out straggling hairs or you will end up with a row of bristles at the top of the mane.

Plait the forelock in exactly the same way. If the horse has a thick forelock, you can clip out a small section where the bridle headpiece goes. If his forelock is sparse, do not clip out any hair but pull a small section of mane through to bulk out your forelock plait.

Clever plaiting can create an optical illusion. If the horse has a weak neck, set the plaits on top to give the impression of more bulk. If his neck is too heavy, set them to the side.

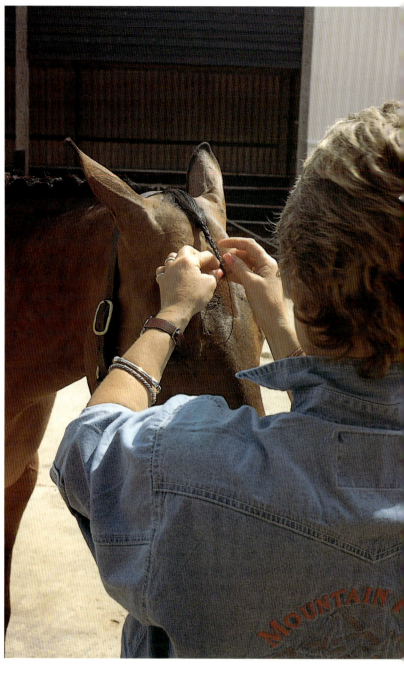

If your horse is slightly short in the neck, more plaits (within reason) create the illusion of extra length. Fewer plaits make an overlong neck look slightly shorter. Sewn-in plaits look neat and will stay in place with the minimum of stitches. Plaiting will not damage the mane but is important to be careful when you remove the plaits; it is too easy to cut mane hair instead of thread.

Use a dressmaker's stitch unpicker rather than scissors. You can hook this through the stitches and break the thread without breaking the mane hair. The mane will be wavy when you undo the plaits, but brushing with a damp brush will soon make it lie flat again (*see opposite*).

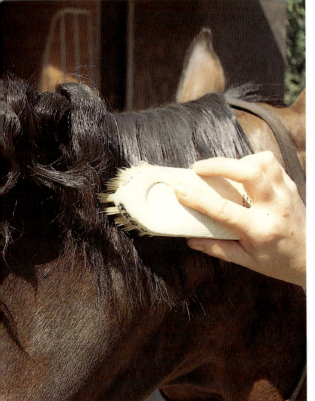

HOLDING POWER

Some event riders plait their horses' manes for the dressage and show-jumping phases but undo all, or just the first two, plaits for the cross-country phase in case they need an emergency handle. Fastening a doubled length of thread through the forelock plait and tying it round the bridle headpiece lessens the risk of the bridle being pulled off in a fall.

BAND AID

With practice, sewn-in plaits are quick to do and in many cases are the only acceptable kind. However, in an emergency you may need to take short cuts and in this situation plaits can be secured with rubber bands.

Plaiting bands are small, strong and available in a wide range of colours. Again, choose the one nearest to the colour of your horse's mane – we have used bands in a different colour to show the technique.

Prepare and section off the mane as for sewn plaits, but when you get to the end of each plait, fasten it with a rubber band. Roll up the plait to the base of the neck and use a second band to keep it in place.

Rubber-band plaits do not look as neat or stay in place as well as sewn ones. They can be useful for a 'dry run' when you want to see how many plaits best suit your horse's conformation.

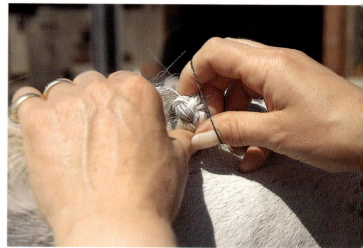

STABLE PLAITS

Stable plaits help to train an unruly mane, or one which has been hogged and is growing out, to lie flat. Divide it into sections and plait down as before, keeping the plaits tight from the base. Fasten with rubber bands and leave in for a couple of days at a time. Repeat frequently.

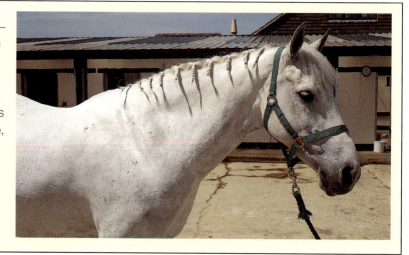

RUNNING AND SPANISH PLAITS

Manes are not always plaited just for decorative reasons, sometimes it is purely practical. If you have an Arab or a native pony who has a long mane, it may get in the way when you are doing fast work or jumping. Ordinary plaits are too bulky for a natural mane, but a running or Spanish plait makes an attractive alternative.

THE RUNNING PLAIT

Comb through the mane so that there are no tangles. For a running plait, take a section near the ears as if you were going to make an ordinary plait. Plait down as before, and take in a small piece of mane as you pass the left-hand section over the centre one.

Continue the plait but, instead of pulling it tight, let the mane fall naturally. Take in a new section of mane every time you pass the left-hand section over. As you progress, the plait will curve round.

Carry on for the full length of the mane, taking in the same amount of hair each time. Eventually you will have one long plait forming the bottom edge of the mane. As you reach the withers and there is no more hair to take in, plait the strands that are left and fasten the ends as you would an ordinary plait. Double up the loose ends and fasten them with thread.

THE SPANISH PLAIT

A Spanish plait is made in a similar way but, instead of curving down and round, it follows the line of the crest. To achieve this effect, plait as before – taking in a new section of hair every time you pass the left section over the centre – but keep the plait pulled tight.

If your horse or pony has a particularly thick mane and you want to keep it out of the way without pulling it, try a double Spanish plait. Make a centre parting down the full length of the mane so that an equal amount of hair falls on each side of the neck, and plait each side separately.

These plaits are often used on Spanish and other parade horses, perhaps with coloured ribbons woven in. Other techniques include ones such as this lattice plait, for vaulting animals, and decorations for heavy horses.

Standard plaits are the only ones currently accepted in the show ring, though running and Spanish plaits are just as attractive. The dressage world is more open-minded and there is an increasing trend for Andalucians and Lusitanos to be turned out for dressage competitions in what is, after all, a traditional way for the breeds.

PLAITING TAILS

PICK YOUR PLAIT

If your horse has a full tail and you do not want to pull it, plaiting the top will emphasise a good pair of hindquarters. However, plaiting a tail well is more difficult than plaiting a mane – and some tails are easier than others!

There are two forms of plaited tail, one where the plait lies flat (1) and the other where it stands out in relief (2). The second kind is more attractive but perhaps a little more difficult.

The hair at the dock must be long enough to get the plait started. The tail must be clean and well brushed out, or specks of white grease will be evident, but preferably washed a couple of days beforehand so that the hair is not too slippery to get hold of and keep tight.

SHOWING OFF

A plaited tail is perfectly acceptable for most showing classes, especially for youngstock. However, if you want to compete at anything above local level you will find that pulled tails are universal in ridden classes. Many producers feel that a plaited tail does not look professional enough.

PLAITING TECHNIQUES

To start your tail plait, take a small section of hair from each side of the tail at the top. Cross them over and take a third section from the side to the centre of the tail, also at the top.

Use a similar technique to that used for a Spanish or running plait, but this time take in extra hairs from *each* side as you pass the sides over the centre section. It is important to keep your plaiting tight, so that the side bars lie flat and taut and the actual plait runs straight down the centre of the tail. Only take in small amounts of hair from the side each time, or the plait will be too thick by the time you reach the bottom.

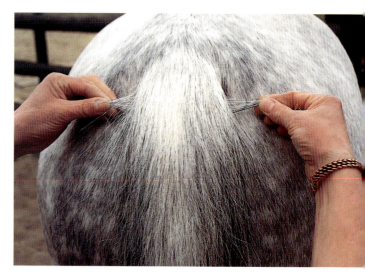

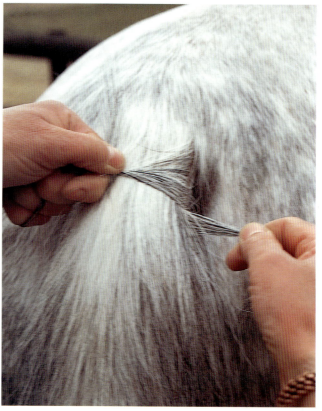

If you want to make a flat plait, pass the side sections over the top of the centre one each time, as if you were plaiting a mane. To create a raised plait, pass them underneath. If you are used to plaiting in the conventional way, this may take a little practice.

Plait down in this way until your centre plait reaches two thirds of the way down the dock. Continue the plait but do not take in any more side hairs so that you end up with a single long plait.

Carry on to the end then fasten with needle and thread as for sewn mane plaits. Double up the loose ends and secure, then pass the needle through the centre of the plait, from the underneath, where the side bars finish. Some people like to leave the loop as it is, whilst others prefer to stitch down its length so that it lies flat. American show riders often finish their plaited tails with a 'pinwheel', rolling the end into a circle and stitching it.

As with mane plaits, resist the temptation to pull out stray hairs. A little hair gel or hairspray can be used to make them lie flat.

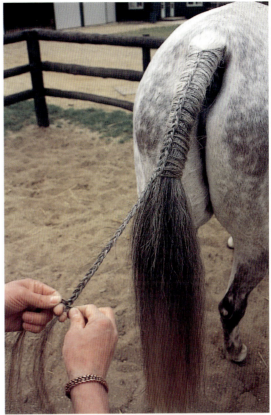

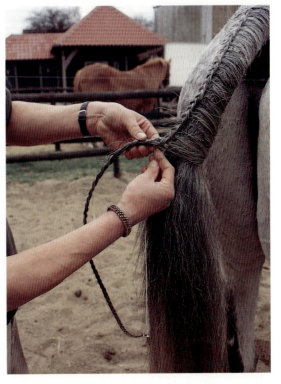

ALL WRAPPED UP

If you are travelling to a show, you will obviously need to protect the tail with a tail bandage. Apply it with care and remove it even more carefully! You will need to unwind it rather than pulling it off from the top, which would damage your plait.

ACKNOWLEDGEMENTS

Thanks to Lynn Russell, Bailey's Showing Team, and Michael Elwick, International League for the Protection of Horses, for their skills in pulling and plaiting and to Sarah Turner for organisation. Thanks also to the equine models, especially Blue, Harry and Luke – all horses who have been rehabilitated by the ILPH – and Merlin.

British Library Cataloguing-in-Publication Data.
A catalogue record for this book is available from the
British Library

ISBN 0.85131.676.X

Published in Great Britain in 1997 by
J. A. Allen & Company Limited,
1 Lower Grosvenor Place, Buckingham Palace Road,
London, SW1W OEL

Design and Typesetting by Paul Saunders
Series editor, Jane Lake
Printed in Hong Kong by Dah Hua Printing Press Co. Ltd.